CAMPFIRE STORIES

CAMPFIRE STORIES

SPOOKY STORIES TO SHARE AND DELIGHT

KELLY ANNE McLELLAN

ROCKRIDGE
PRESS

First Rockridge Press trade paperback edition 2022

Rockridge Press and the Rockridge Press logo are trademarks or registered trademarks of Callisto Media Inc. and/or its affiliates in the United States and other countries and may not be used without written permission.

For general information on our other products and services, please contact our Customer Care Department within the United States at (866) 744-2665, or outside the United States at (510) 253-0500.

Paperback ISBN: 978-1-68539-428-8 | eBook ISBN: 978-1-68539-968-9

Manufactured in the United States of America

Interior and Cover Designer: Joshua Moore and Lindsey Dekker
Art Producer: Melissa Malinowsky
Editor: Barbara J. Isenberg
Production Editor: Cassie Gitkin
Production Manager: Lanore Coloprisco

All illustrations used under license from iStock; icons used under license from Noun Project; author photo courtesy of Kathryn McRae Photography.

10 9 8 7 6 5 4 3 2 1 0

CONTENTS

✦ WELCOME, READERS! ✦

Telling stories around a campfire is a time-honored tradition and one I am excited to share with you. This book is full of amazing stories you can read by yourself or out loud. Whether you're in your living room with a fake construction paper fire or out in the woods camping with your family, you'll love getting goose bumps during the spookiest parts of these stories or laughing loudly with those around you at the funny scenes.

There are NO rules in this book. Feel free to read these stories one after the other, or skip around. Reading is meant to be fun and enjoyable, so *you* get to choose this adventure.

Many stories you're about to read are similar to the stories your grandparents told around a campfire when they were your age. I've had the honor of updating them to include technology and modern-day settings.

So what are you waiting for? It's time to get started! Which story do you want to read first? The choice is all yours.

Happy reading!
Kelly Anne

The Ashes in the Fire

The summer I turned nine was a big milestone. I finally got to go to summer camp. With a mix of excitement and dread, I packed my gear. For years my older brother had told me horror stories of campers being carried away in the night by ghosts or eaten by wild animals! I was nervous, but I wasn't going to chicken out. I was ready to spend a week in the woods at Camp Desolation.

My first day went well. Swimming, archery, and camp crafts occupied my mind. Even the camp food wasn't as bad as my brother had described.

But as the sun began to set, I felt the hair stand up on the back of my neck. Before I knew it, the sky was surprisingly dark, much darker than it got at home.

The stars overhead twinkled more brightly than I had ever seen back in our city neighborhood. All my senses were heightened as the other kids and I filed down the trail to the council fire. I could smell the burning wood, and soon the flickering flames were visible.

We spoke in hushed voices as we sat around the fire and were greeted by a senior camper wearing all black. "Tonight," he told us, "we will be joined by the spirits that have come before us. Before you were even born, they were sitting around this very same campfire."

My imagination raced. There *were* ghosts at Camp Desolation! They were coming to visit us. Tonight! The stories were true! My heart beat a little faster, and my palms got sweaty.

The older kid then produced a bag and

slowly poured what looked like ashes into the flames. They crackled into the fire.

Were these the bones of the campers before us? Was I going to be next? Every instinct told me to run before it was too late, but I was frozen in place. I wanted to move—to run and hide—but I was even more scared of leaving and missing out on this opportunity of a lifetime. I took a few deep breaths to calm down and listened carefully to the words the senior camper was saying.

Suddenly, I began to understand. I had it all wrong. These weren't bones! They were only ashes from previous campfires collected at the end of evenings past. As the older kid recounted the many years of tradition, I realized that I was connected to generations of campers who had come before me. *I was a part of the spirit of the camp.*

In that moment, summer camp no longer seemed so scary. I knew I would be able to relax and enjoy my time there. Then I remembered ghost stories were coming up next, and I got scared all over again!

The Drenched Campers

Throughout the years, campers avoided Lake Highline in Grand Junction, Colorado. From one generation to another, stories were handed down that the lake mysteriously "called" young children into it. For some unknown reason, children would get stuck in a trance and walk directly into the lake, never resurfacing.

Eventually, though, memories faded. Over the years Lake Highline became a great place to spend the hot summers. During the day, lifeguards were stationed near the lake's access points. In the evenings, they even roamed the beaches. Nobody knew why a lake would need lifeguards while everyone was sleeping. That is, until the weekend the Blakely-Chen family decided to visit.

It was a hot and busy weekend. The Blakely-Chen family was excited to kick back, relax, and enjoy their weekend. Jake, Jasper, and their dads gathered around the campfire the first night, telling spooky stories. Mr. Blakely, who had grown up in a small town nearby, decided to tell the terrifying history of Lake Highline. As he shared the spooky stories, his family looked around nervously, firelight flicking over their faces. Could this happen to them?

It came time for bed, and everyone walked back to their tents through the dewy grass. A few moments later, Mr. Blakely heard his husband screaming, "Jake! Jasper! Where are you?"

An urgent search began, but it didn't last long. "There!" someone shouted. Somehow, the boys had traveled to the other side of the lake in mere minutes. They were standing on the far shore, walking into the water. They looked like robots, moving stiffly and in sync, marching toward the lake's depths step-by-step. The fastest way to reach them was through the lake, so Mr. Blakely and Mr. Chen both dove in, trying to swim to their boys as quickly as possible. Fellow campers heard the splashes and kicking, terrified. Suddenly it was eerily silent, and nobody could see or hear anything from the shoreline.

The lifeguards and other campers searched through the night, but they couldn't find the Blakely-Chen family anywhere. When it came time to pack up the next day, nobody knew what to do with their camping equipment. A friend decided to clean it up and store it for them, hoping that the family would be found and could use the equipment in the future, unlikely as that was. When she pulled back the opening of the tent, she found Jake, Jasper, and their dads inside, all of them sopping wet and fast asleep.

THE RINGING OF
THE BELLS

Many years ago, a deadly plague moved from one town to another. People died quickly, and a doctor wasn't always nearby to officially declare a patient dead. The bodies were buried, but sometimes it was too soon. Once in a while a body was buried . . . alive.

For safety, the villagers put a string in each coffin, with a bell at the other end. All day and night, someone sat in the graveyard listening for a faint *ring . . . ring . . .* which meant someone was buried alive and needed help!

Twelve-year-old Jeremiah was responsible for maintaining his family's cemetery. Every

7

day he walked the grounds, making sure the property was tidy.

Jeremiah thought of buried people as part of his family. He especially liked Mrs. Mathias, who died years before Jeremiah was born. Her tombstone said she was kind and always helped others.

Mrs. Mathias had died after stopping to help an old man whose foot was stuck in a hole. He was stubborn and refused her help. When Mrs. Mathias didn't give up, he grabbed her and hit her over the head with his cane. She died immediately and was buried there, in the graveyard.

Sitting next to her tombstone comforted Jeremiah and gave him a perfect view of the cemetery. He laid a blanket near Mrs. Mathias, settled in, and closed his eyes, listening for the sound of a bell. Most nights were quiet, but one night he heard a noise coming from the road. "*Uggghhhhhh.*" It sounded like someone was struggling and needed help. Jeremiah looked around but couldn't see anyone or anything.

"*Unnnnhhhhhh*," the voice said again.

Slowly, Jeremiah crept toward the road. The night sky made it hard to see where the voice was coming from. As his eyes adjusted in the shadows, Jeremiah saw an old man. His foot was wedged tightly in a pothole along the walking path.

"Oh no!" Jeremiah cried. "Let me help you."

The old man looked up with an evil smirk. "Why can't you leave me alone? Always getting in the way!" Then the old man grabbed Jeremiah, terrifying him.

Suddenly, the sound of a bell ringing fast and loud filled the air, startling the old man and Jeremiah. The old man let go of Jeremiah and stumbled away. Jeremiah rushed back to the cemetery, searching over the freshly dug graves, looking for the ringing bell. To his surprise, the ringing sound was coming from the direction of his blanket. Jeremiah tiptoed to his favorite spot and saw that the ringing was coming from the grave of Mrs. Mathias.

The Hook

Julius and Tyrone arrived at their wooded campsite, excited to unload their supplies and set up camp. But soon, dark clouds rolled in and the skies opened up. Lightning and thunder forced them into their tent. Their hopes of playing in the woods and exploring the nearby creek vanished.

In the tent, they played card games, listened to the radio, and talked about their plans for later, after the rain stopped.

As the hours passed and the rain continued, Julius and Tyrone grew bored.

"Want to tell some scary stories?" Julius asked as he climbed into his sleeping bag to get comfy.

"Yes!" replied Tyrone. "It's the perfect night for scary stories."

"Have you ever heard the one about the hook?" Julius asked.

Tyrone shook his head no.

"Oh good. It's a classic! Years ago, a man with a hook for a hand escaped from the local prison. He roamed around our town for hours, tormenting anyone he could find. He would use his hook to make scratching noises on the sides of cars, on doors, or on windows to get people to come out. Then he would attack them with his hook and cut off their hands—so that they would have a hook for a hand, too."

Tyrone's eyes grew wide, and Julius smiled. He knew he had done a good job telling the story because his friend was spooked! He turned off the flashlight and lay down.

Suddenly there was a scratching noise coming from the side of the tent. *Scratchhhh . . .*

Both boys jumped out of their sleeping bags, startled.

Scratchhhh . . . It definitely wasn't in their heads.

Something—or someone—was scratching at their tent.

"No way am I opening this tent!" whispered Tyrone.

"Me either. Maybe we better leave the scary stories for another time."

Rattled and nervous, both boys decided it was time to sleep. Eventually, they drifted off, listening to the rain patter on the tent.

The next morning, the rain had stopped. The boys could finally get on with their camping activities. As they gathered wood and splashed in the creek, they forgot about the scratching from the night before.

It wasn't until they returned to their campsite with armfuls of firewood that Julius thought about investigating the tent to see if the scratching had left any marks.

To their shock and horror, hanging from the back of the tent was a shiny . . . silver . . . HOOK!

The Underpants

After Mr. Davis passed away, Mrs. Davis struggled to adjust to her new normal. Every day she went about her routine, taking care of their old home in the woods. She was used to washing Mr. Davis's clothes, making his meals, and helping him with his daily tasks. Now that it was just her, she felt silly going about her day. She didn't need much for her simple life.

While alive, Mr. Davis had also been a simple man with only two pairs of underpants and a few modest outfits. He liked to eat the same meals every day for breakfast, lunch, and dinner. When he passed, Mrs. Davis buried Mr. Davis in an outfit he'd worn every week for as long as she could remember. She didn't

know
what to
do with his
other pair
of under-
pants or his
old clothes, so for
now, they stayed in his
dresser until she could find a
good use for them.

Late one night, not long after he'd died, Mrs. Davis was startled awake by the presence of someone else in her room. Her heart was racing, and her entire body tensed up. She couldn't believe it, but standing at the end of her bed was the ghost of her husband. She shut her eyes tight, wishing him away. Of course, she missed her husband, but having his spirit visit her in the middle of the night wasn't her idea of fun.

"Shoo!" she muttered from the comfort of her bed. "Get out of here!" But against her wishes, the ghost returned every night for a month, disrupting her sleep and scaring her awake, night after night. Finally, Mrs. Davis got tired of being woken up, so she packed up the house and moved closer to the city. She even brought her husband's dresser of clothes, because she wasn't ready to get rid of them yet.

But Mr. Davis was persistent. He found her in the city as well and continued to visit her every night. So Mrs. Davis moved again. And again. And again! But it didn't work. Mr. Davis still showed up at the foot of her bed every night.

Finally, instead of wishing her husband's ghost away, she decided she'd had enough. That night when Mr. Davis visited, Mrs. Davis sat right up and demanded, "What the heck are you doing here?" He looked back at her in earnest and said, "Where's my other pair of underpants? I can't wear the same pair forever."

A Little
More Room

Matthew was listening to his favorite podcast as he walked to school. A chill suddenly came over him, giving him goose bumps. He turned down his podcast and stopped, looking around. That's when a car pulled up in front of him, screeching to a halt. Matthew's heart raced, and the horrible feeling sank deeper into his bones.

The driver rolled down his window and leaned toward Matthew. His smile was genuine and inviting. "Good morning, sir. Would you like a ride to school? I've got a little more room." The man pointed to the back, and that's when Matthew noticed it wasn't a regular car. It was a hearse! He could clearly see a coffin resting in the back.

Matthew couldn't explain it, but something about this man's voice relaxed him. It was as if he was supposed to follow this man, no matter what. Matthew knew to never take rides from strangers, so why did he feel so strange?

"Errr . . . I . . . no, thank you," Matthew managed to stutter. As quickly as it had arrived, the hearse was gone. The sinking feeling in Matthew's body slowly melted away, and he felt like himself again. He turned his podcast back up and continued on his way.

By the time he reached school, it was as if nothing had happened. Matthew walked through the lobby to the elevator. The doors were closing, and Matthew felt the horrible sinking feeling come over his body again. A hand reached out and stopped the closing doors.

"Would you like to join me? I've got a little more room." The same man from the hearse was on the elevator!

Again, even though Matthew wanted nothing to do with this man, a powerful force was drawing him in. Matthew felt his feet begin to step forward. With all his might, he stopped and said, "Oops! I forgot something." Before his body could change his mind, he turned and sprinted away.

He heard the elevator doors shut behind him, and the feeling of dread left him.

Suddenly, a horrible *BANG* rang out. Matthew turned back and saw smoke and dust pouring out of the cracks of the elevator doors. It was hours before anyone knew exactly what had happened, but Matthew felt a bizarre sense of peace all day. Finally, the principal came over the loudspeaker to talk about the elevator.

"I am sad to share that the elevator cables snapped, and the car plunged to the basement."

Matthew felt a rush of relief—and also sadness. He didn't know the man in the elevator, but he had seemed nice.

The principal continued. "If anyone had been inside, they would have died. Luckily, the elevator was empty."

The Two Heads

The taxi driver pulled up to 123 Cottage Lane at exactly 1:23 p.m. to pick up Jackie Breeze. She was heading to the airport and had two old suitcases with her. As the driver got out of the car to open the trunk, he quickly realized a horrible stench was coming from the two suitcases. He turned his nose and grimaced, but Mrs. Breeze gave him a pointed look that told him not to mention the smell. He quickly changed his expression, remembering his tip, and placed the wretched suitcases in the trunk.

He got in the car and immediately had to roll down the window. The stench was wafting into the front seat from the trunk, making him feel nauseated. Jackie snapped at him, insisting that he roll the window up. The driver was starting to wish he had just stayed home in bed. Not only was the smell awful, but Jackie Breeze was giving off a horrible vibe. The driver felt more and more anxious with every passing mile.

What in the world could be in those suit-cases? the driver thought. *Rotten eggs, maybe? But why on Earth would anyone carry around rotten eggs?*

What about stinky gym clothes? he wondered. No, he decided. The smell was far too horrible to be dirty laundry, no matter how old or stinky it may be.

Suddenly his face grew white. What if it was something really bad? Like a human head? Or a rotten hand? It had to be something completely horrid. He couldn't imagine what else would produce the rotten stench he was trying with all his might to ignore.

No longer caring about his tip, the

driver drove to the airport as fast and reck-lessly as possible in hopes of shortening the ride. He was determined to get the horrendous smell out of his car and put this experience behind him as soon as possible.

His taxi screamed into the parking lot. Then he popped the trunk and ran around to grab the suitcases. He couldn't wait to have the rotten stench out of his car and far away. In his haste, he pulled too hard. The weak locks snapped and both suitcases dropped open before he could set them on the ground. To his absolute horror, two rotting heads rolled out onto the ground—

A head of lettuce and a head of cabbage.

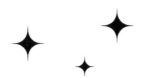

The Dream Fairies

One evening, when I was a small child, I lay awake in bed. Storm clouds circled outside my window, and the wind howled through the trees, creating a dreadful sound. The stars had disappeared, and the once-warm glow of the moon was now nothing more than an eerie shape hiding behind dark, swirling clouds. I was terrified to go to sleep—I didn't want bad dreams to sneak in. When my mom came to say good night, I told her about my fears. She gently sat at the end of the bed and rubbed my back. That was when she told me all about the dream fairies, and why I shouldn't worry . . . or should I?

"Do you ever wonder how dreams enter your mind?" my mom asked me. "Between being awake and deeply asleep, there is a moment when the dream fairies arrive to plant a seed in every child's head. That seed grows into the dream world we experience while we sleep."

"But what dream will grow from that seed?" I asked.

"It depends," she replied. "It depends on whether you've been good during the day. The fairies watch everything we do, from the highest corner in each room to the blooms of nearby flowers."

"What do they see?" I asked.

"They see how you behave. Good little boys and girls will have happy dreams and silly dreams. But kids who misbehave . . ." My mother paused and clucked her tongue.

"What happens if we misbehave?" I asked in a wavering voice.

"Let's not think about that, my love," she said.

It was hard not to notice the concern in her voice. My mind raced as I thought back on my day.

Had I been nice to everyone? Had I tried my best to stay out of trouble?

Yes. That particular day I had been on my best behavior. I went to sleep with trust in my mom's word—but not before I made a note to do something nice for a friend the next day.

As you probably will, I often stop and question my mom's story. But I offer a word of caution. Do you dare risk the night terrors? Or do you play it safe?

Whatever you decide, tonight, when you are lying in bed, nearly asleep, look for that faint shimmer of light in the darkness and know that the dream fairies are coming for you. Will your night be cheerful, or will it be full of the unthinkable? You have chosen your path!

Clap Clap

They entered the deep Colorado canyon with bright moonlight leading the way. Aalina and Tan were searching for the elusive elf owl, a nocturnal creature that was difficult to find.

Their footsteps echoed loudly in the canyon. Every few minutes, they would stop and listen for the distinctive sound of the elf owl, a yapping call that was surprisingly loud for such a tiny creature.

After finally reaching a wide, flat rock, they waited for their eyes to adjust to their dark surroundings. Every second, their view became clearer. Eventually they could see the Milky Way and the prickly cacti looming around them.

After twenty minutes, they clearly heard the distinct yapping call of the elf owl, letting them know there was one nearby. Without even thinking, Aalina and Tan rushed off in the direction of the sound. They followed it from one place to the next, barely glimpsing an owl as it swooped down into the canyon to grab its prey. The noise of the calls got so loud, there had to be twenty or more owls flying around them. It drowned out everything else.

Finally, Tan called it quits. "I am exhausted. I think it's time to head back."

"I agree," Aalina said, letting out a breath.

They looked around and suddenly realized they had no idea where they were! They began wandering, unsure of where to go. After an hour of not making progress, Aalina and Tan decided it was time to sit down and stay put. In the morning, their parents would come to find them.

They settled into the canyon and slowly drooped, succumbing to exhaustion. Just as they reached a light sleep, they heard a loud *CLAP*.

Aalina jolted awake. "What?"

Clap, clap. They heard it again. Now Tan was wide awake, too.

"Hello?" he called. "Who's there?"

Another *clap* echoed through the canyon. Both kids looked around but couldn't see anything. The echo made it impossible to know where the noise was coming from.

"Maybe it's someone who can't talk," suggested Tan.

Aalina pondered that, then called out, "Can you hear us? Clap once for yes and twice for no."

Clap.

"Okay . . . so weird," said Tan.

Aalina nodded in agreement and continued.

"We're lost. Can you help us?"

Clap. Clap.

Tan and Aalina looked at each other, puzzled. "Are you lost too?"

Clap. Clap.

Now they were curious. "Do you live here?"

Clap. Clap.

"Are you a kid?"

Clap. Clap.

"Are you an adult?"

Clap. Clap.

With a shaky breath, Aalina asked, "Are you human?"

Clap. Clap.

Terrified, Aalina and Tan each grabbed a stick from the ground and slowly stood up, holding hands.

"How many of you are there?" Tan finally asked.

Clap. Clap.

The Scarecrows

Every autumn, the Moog family set out their new scarecrows in the fields, knowing they would all be gone by winter. They were never sure what happened to them or where they went, but the scarecrows would always disappear one night during the planting season.

The Moogs were frustrated—scarecrows weren't cheap or easy to make, and each of their five fields needed one to keep pests away. But year after year, they kept disappearing.

They had theories. The oldest Moogs thought their friends were playing tricks on them. The younger Moogs thought monsters saw the scarecrows as a threat and came to eat them. But the most level-headed daughter of the Moog family, Logan, thought there was a rational reason that the scarecrows went missing. Maybe it was the weather, or perhaps some sort of critter—whatever it was, she wanted to get to the bottom of it this year.

Logan told her family that she would watch the fields all night long until she saw what happened to their scarecrows. She would sleep during the day and be the night guard during the long evenings.

For an entire month, Logan stayed up all night. Whenever she joined her family for their dinner—her breakfast—they all made fun of her.

"There are still five scarecrows out there! What were you thinking?"

But Logan was determined not to give up. Finally, her tenacity was rewarded. It was an extra-dark night, with almost no moon. Everything was eerily quiet. Logan was stationed near the window watching the fields, just like she had done every night for a month. Suddenly a horrible feeling came over her. She felt angry—not like herself at all. Then, from the corner of her eye, she thought she saw something move. Logan glanced over and noticed that one of the scarecrows seemed farther away than it had been before.

Through the darkness, Logan squinted to focus on the scarecrow. It didn't appear to be moving, but the scarecrow *was* shrinking, right before her eyes. Was it moving farther away? Or getting smaller? Logan wanted to run out into the field and investigate, but she was also terrified and confused. She struggled to focus.

Finally, needing to know the truth, Logan gathered her courage and sprinted from the window, down the stairs, and out the front door. The second her feet hit the grass, she knew. All five scarecrows were already gone. To this day, she'll never know where they went or how they disappeared. But Logan decided she didn't need to know—no matter what the cause, the Moogs would have to accept losing their scare-crows, year after year.

The Late-Night Abduction

S hondra was fast asleep in her bed as the spaceship hovered silently next to her window. A door in the spaceship opened. A shaft of light came out of the opening, focusing on Shondra. She silently rose into the air, sleeping soundly, and the beam sucked her into the spaceship. Nobody witnessed it, and her parents didn't hear anything, even though they were in the room next door.

The aliens on board the spaceship were shorter than the average human and had pale gray skin, large oval heads, and big black eyes. They were excited about their new specimen and couldn't wait to see what they could learn from her.

The spaceship traveled light-years away. Once it reached its destination, Planet X, the aliens gently unloaded Shondra from the spaceship. Shondra had been sound asleep until then, and the jostling was enough to stir her.

"*AHHH!*" Shondra screamed. "WHERE AM I? WHO ARE YOU?"

The aliens used their stubby arms to hold her upright, but they didn't answer or say anything. In fact, they had no idea what she was saying. They only spoke their planet's language, which was not English.

The aliens gently carried Shondra into their laboratory and strapped her down. They ran an X-ray machine over her, took a quick blood sample, and plucked several hairs from her head. The whole time, Shondra was screaming and pleading for them to let her go. But the aliens acted like this was completely normal and kept on working.

Quickly moving back to their spaceship

with Shondra at their sides, the aliens loaded her back up. They returned their ship to planet Earth, and navigated toward Shondra's home. Before they sent her back to her own bed, they held up an item that looked a lot like a flashlight and shined it in her eyes. Shondra stopped screaming and fighting immediately. She simply lay down and started softly snoring. Then the spaceship door opened back up, light poured out onto Shondra's window, and Shondra floated like a feather back into her bed.

According to the clock in her room, Shondra had only been gone for fifteen minutes. When she woke up the next morning, she felt a little more sleepy than usual, like she had been running in place the whole night. But she had no memory of anything else ever happening.

The Ghost of the Bloody Finger

Kids at the local elementary school told many tales about the old house at the edge of the neighborhood. It stood abandoned for hundreds of years. Everyone told the story differently, but they all agreed they heard a voice coming from that house whenever they were near its front yard.

Eight-year-old Lachlan was walking past the house one day with his younger brother Orion when they heard someone whisper from the porch. They both stopped and stood still, straining to make out the words and hardly believing their ears at the same time. The soft speaking went on, but the boys couldn't understand what it said. After a minute of trying to find the source of the whisper, they got spooked and ran home as fast as their legs could carry them. The next day, they walked past the house and heard something again. Both boys had taken just one step forward when an eerie voice made them freeze where they stood. "I am the ghost of the bloody finger!" they heard this time. Lachlan and Orion looked at each other, the color draining from their faces. Out of the shadows, a pale man appeared.

"*AAAAAAAAGHHH!*" they screamed, then quickly bolted away.

That night both boys were so scared they couldn't sleep. "We have to find out what is going on," Orion said, determined.

"I agree," Lachlan concluded. The next day, they gathered their courage and slowly walked past the house. They couldn't see or hear anyone, so they cautiously opened the creaky gate and stepped onto the property.

"Hello?" Lachlan's voice squeaked. "Anyone here?" Nobody answered. The boys walked deeper into the garden until the path disappeared and they couldn't see beyond the bushes.

"Wait!" Orion whispered, holding out his arm to stop Lachlan. "Look." Several feet in front of them, crouched under a bush, was the pale figure from the previous day. He was bent over, holding his own hand. The boys bravely inched closer. It was a ghost, all right, and a thick puddle of blood was forming at his feet.

The ghost slowly raised his head and made eye contact with the boys. They were stuck in place and couldn't move, terrified.

"I am the ghost of the bloody finger," the ghost bellowed again. "Could I borrow a Band-Aid, please?"

Hide-and-Seek Nightmares

Every summer, Julia and Ginny went to the beach with their family. The house they rented year after year was large enough for their entire family. There was even a basement with plenty of extra rooms—or so they were told. Every year, they asked if they could use the basement, but the owners insisted that nobody ever go down there. They said the basement flooded and wasn't safe to stay in. Julia and Ginny found it odd, but the rest of the house was large enough for everyone.

The first three days of vacation this year were just like every other. At the beach, the entire family played in the waves, looked for seashells, and built a sprawling sandcastle with a large moat around it.

The fourth day was different. A massive storm blew in overnight, and the waves were huge. The wind howled against the windows, and rain spilled from the clouds nonstop.

Julia and Ginny didn't let the bad weather dampen their spirits. They decided to play the most epic game of hide-and-seek ever.

After a few rounds, they were running out of new places to hide, so when Ginny covered her eyes and started counting, she wasn't surprised to hear footsteps quietly descending the stairs into the basement.

"Ready or not, here I come!" Ginny shouted, taking off down the stairs. She had never been to the basement, so she was shocked when she reached the bottom step and the atmosphere suddenly changed. The air was cooler and quieter. She couldn't hear any of the waves or the wind above, and she instantly got the chills. But she was pretty sure that Julia was down here, too, so she pushed forward.

Along the hallway, there were at least ten doors on either side. Ginny slowly opened each one, briefly looked around, then quietly closed the door. Every room was damp, dark, and entirely empty. The only light was near the top of the stairs, so the farther she explored, the darker it became.

When she opened the sixth door, Ginny saw a cupboard sitting in the middle of the room. The cabinet door was rocking back and forth slightly, like someone had recently touched it. She leaped forward, yelling, "Aha! I found you."

But when she opened the door, she gasped. Yes, Julia was there . . . but only half of her. She was holding onto the cupboard for dear life with her hands, while her bottom half was being pulled into a black vortex in the back of the cupboard. She looked like she was scream-

ing, but Ginny couldn't hear anything. Ginny grabbed Julia's hands and pulled with all her might, but Julia only slipped farther back into the cupboard.

Ginny pulled and pulled and pulled. She could feel Julia fighting, even though she couldn't hear anything. Julia's body twisted side to side like she was kicking and trying to crawl her way out of the cupboard.

Eventually, Ginny felt Julia budge a little, so she pulled harder and got a little more leverage. She gave one last tug with every ounce of energy left, and *POP!* Julia was free and tumbled out onto Ginny.

Without another word, both girls got up, realized they were okay, and ran up the stairs swiftly and silently. They never spoke of the incident ever again.

Stinky Feet Really Stink

Every year Isla's town held a Stinky Shoe Competition. Isla's family went every year, and they loved watching the judges' faces as they smelled each pair of ridiculously stinky shoes. When Isla was finally old enough, she decided it was her turn to enter. But she didn't want to just enter it. Isla wanted to win the Stinky Shoe Competition.

Isla bought a comfy pair of gym shoes to make as stinky as possible. For an entire year, Isla did everything she could to stink up the shoes. She ran miles in the scorching sun. She walked through algae in the nearby pond. And she never once washed her feet!

As the year wore on, the shoes became less and less comfortable, but Isla was determined to win. So the shoes never came off. Not even to sleep.

Isla's friends and family began to stay away from Isla and her stinky shoes. But Isla didn't care. She wanted to win the gold medal!

On the day of the competition, Isla was so excited. The shoes were so stinky, the crowd parted as she walked to the stage!

Two other kids with stinky feet were competing against her, but Isla knew they didn't stand a chance. The judges lined up, and the contestants stuck out their feet. Each judge slowly sniffed the first contestant's shoe and grimaced. What a smell!

They moved on to contestant number two and took a big whiff. One of the judges gagged, and another's eyes began to water.

Then it was Isla's turn. As the judges bent over to smell Isla's shoes, they turned away instantly. One judge fainted. Another judge ran away with her hand over her mouth. And the last judge pinched their nose and announced Isla the clear winner of this year's Stinky Shoe Competition!

Isla was so excited! But no one would celebrate with her because her feet were so stinky! Now that she had won, Isla decided it was time for the smelly shoes to finally come off.

But as Isla skipped home, she felt a tingling inside her shoes. Then her toes started to itch. The itching slowly worked its way up to her ankles, until Isla couldn't even feel her feet anymore.

As she tore off the prized shoes, Isla looked down and gasped in horror. Her feet had completely melted away inside her shoes!

Silver Dollar Thank-You

think we need to stop!" Harper shouted to Charlie through the pouring rain. She could only see a few feet in front of her as they pedaled home from a day at the river.

Charlie twirled his lucky silver dollar between his fingers and slowed to a stop. "You're right!" he yelled. "This doesn't feel safe at all." Pointing up the hill to an old house, Charlie asked, "Think we can stop in there?"

"Anything is better than staying out here," Harper said.

They pedaled through the wind and rain to the old house on the hill. The light in the windows welcomed them, and they knew this was the right choice.

They knocked on the front door. An older woman answered, saw Harper and Charlie standing in the rain with their bikes, and quickly ushered them inside.

Once inside, they could barely hear the rain and wind. A fire warmed the living room, and a young girl was sitting in front of the fireplace playing a card game. The woman brought the children some towels and hot chocolate, and everyone sat next to the fire while they slowly warmed up and dried off.

Harper and Charlie called their worried parents so that the old woman could speak to them. She offered to let the kids stay the night. Their parents wanted to come pick them up right away, but it was too dangerous to drive in the storm.

So Harper and Charlie spent the rest of the night playing cards with the woman and her daughter, eating a large, delicious dinner, and sleeping soundly in warm beds.

They woke up and had a fantastic break-fast with rolls, sausages, and orange juice. They offered to pay the kind old lady, but she and her daughter insisted on accepting nothing. As they were getting ready to leave, Charlie felt compelled to leave something. He took out his lucky silver dollar and gently placed it on the table by the door as a thank-you.

The bike ride home was much safer and calmer this time around. The children arrived at Harper's house in no time. Harper's parents were outside waiting with a big hug when they got there.

"Where is this amazing old woman and her daughter?" asked Harper's mom. "I need to thank them for taking such great care of you two."

"It's just the old house at the top of the hill, right outside town!" Charlie explained. Silently, Harper's parents looked at each other with wide eyes.

"What do you mean? That house burned down when we were kids. It must have been thirty years ago. There was a mother and daughter inside . . . they both died."

"No way!" Harper said. "You must be thinking of a different house."

"Okay, well, why don't you take me there and introduce me?"

Charlie and Harper easily guided Harper's parents to the house on the hill, but as they cleared the crest, everything was different. The inviting home from the night before was now an overgrown shell of a house, completely charred inside and out, and had obviously been that way for many years.

"What . . ." whispered Charlie.

"No. No way." Harper insisted.

They rushed to the house's threshold. There, next to the place where the front door had once stood, was Charlie's lucky silver dollar, shining brightly in the rubble.

The Mysterious Fog

Pattie O'Connor was looking forward to spending the summer in Ireland with her grandad on his sheep farm.

On the plane, she read a book about ancient Irish stories. She loved looking through the pages and studying the pictures of fairies, leprechauns, and banshees.

What is a banshee? Pattie wondered as she found a picture of a pale woman with blood-shot eyes. "The banshee is a horrible omen," she read. "The terrifying woman, wearing all white, screams shortly before a family member dies. Only a few Irish families can hear her: the O'Connors, O'Neills . . ."

The O'Connors? Pattie thought. *I'm an O'Connor! How exciting!*

When Pattie and her parents arrived at the family farm, Pattie sprinted out of the car to hug Grandad. They took off to visit the sheep.

Later that night, everyone fell into a deep sleep, exhausted from traveling. Pattie woke up in the middle of the night, thirsty. She sleepily looked out the window as she filled up her glass and saw thick, fast-moving fog rolling in along the hillside.

When Pattie got up the next day, she thought the farm would be covered in fog. But it was completely clear outside, and the sun was making its way over the hills.

At breakfast, Pattie told her parents about the strange fog she had seen. The color drained from her grandad's face. With a shaky voice, he said, "Wee lass, it was probably the sheep. You must have been seeing things."

"Maybe," Pattie responded. Then she remembered that she and her grandad had put the sheep in the back pasture the night before. It couldn't have been the sheep she saw, could it?

Pattie kept busy with farm chores. Two weeks passed, and she forgot about the weird fog.

One night, Pattie stayed up late, drawing at her desk near the window. The bright light of the full moon lit up the farmland. Pattie looked down at her paper to finish a sketch, and when she looked up again, the same thick fog was rolling in along the countryside. This time, it wasn't alone.

A woman, dressed in white, was gliding in with the fog. Though she was far away, Pattie could see she was ghostly pale with terrifying red eyes. Her mouth opened eerily, and she let out a scream so loud and rattling that Pattie pressed her hands to her ears to try to block it out.

Pattie took off running down the hall. Her book of ancient Irish stories filled her mind. She remembered that only a few Irish families could see and hear the banshees, including her own! She felt a lump in her throat as she remembered the meaning of a banshee's scream.

"GRANDAD!" she yelled, pushing open his bedroom door. But Grandad didn't move. He was lying in bed, dead.

ABOUT THE AUTHOR

 **Kelly Anne McLellan** graduated with a degree in elementary education from the University of South Carolina. She has been a teacher since 2010, and has taught students in Colorado, South Carolina, and Spain, in addition to her many online students from around the world. During the early days of her teaching career, she discovered that she really enjoys helping students fall in love with reading and writing, which still influences every aspect of her work. She welcomed her first son in late 2018 and twin son and daughter in 2020. As a mom, most of her days are spent chasing after her three children and sneaking in time to create curriculums for educators and parents when she can. She lives in Wilmington, North Carolina, with her family.

CPSIA information can be obtained
at www.ICGtesting.com
Printed in the USA
BVHW012109270623
666416BV00003B/18